Child Lines

THE FAMOUS REVEAL THEIR CHILDHOOD DREAMS

RINGPRESS BOOKS
THE GARDEN CITY PUBLISHER

Peter Langridge would like to thank Marion Brett, Jean Wallace, Neil Langridge, Lisa Langridge, Robert Evans and Sally Shore.

Published by Ringpress Books 1989.

An imprint of Ringpress Limited, Spirella House, Bridge Road, Letchworth, Herts SG6 4ET

ISBN 094 8955 80 5

Typeset by Area Graphics Ltd,
Arden Press Way,
Letchworth,
Hertfordshire SG6 1LH

ChildLine

0800 1111

ChildLine, the free national helpline for children in trouble or danger.

For further information about ChildLine send a S.A.E. to ChildLine, 50 Studd Street, London N1 0QJ.

If you would like to make a donation to ChildLine please send it to ChildLine, Freepost 1111, London N1 0BR.

FOREWORD

By ESTHER RANTZEN

THERE are some delicious surprises in this book.

It is a collection of some of the world's most successful and famous people's childhood ambitions – their answer to the question "When you were a child, what did you want to be when you grew up?" The replies are fascinating – and quite unpredictable. For example, you might have guessed that Margaret Thatcher when she was a little girl dreamed of joining the Indian Civil Service. You might even have thought that as a toddler Mikhail Gorbachov wanted to be a farmer. But would you really believe that a tiny Neil Kinnock's ambition was to be a policeman? Or that Sir Peter Hall wished he could become an aeroplane designer? Or Sir Harry Secombe's childhood dream was to be a tap-dancer, only he kept falling into the sink? The world has lost a formidable tap-dancer but gained a wonderful tenor voice, and at least our sinks are safe.

Some of these infant ambitions are more understandable than others. Any little girl can sympathise with Pru Leith who wanted to marry a horse, but personally I cannot imagine how Anna Ford could ever have dreamed of being a saint when she grew up – saints have such very uncomfortable lives, hearing voices, or being pierced with arrows. It says much for her high principles and unswerving courage that she could even contemplate the idea. These confessions are not simply entertaining, they are revealing as well. Many of the singers and comedians tended to know very clearly what they wanted to be when they grew up – and doubtless put in years of practice as children before they found fame and fortune. A number of entertainers admit they never wanted to grow up – and in a way they never have.

Certainly everyone who contributed to this book cares about children, because the profits will go to ChildLine, the national free helpline for children in trouble and danger – children whose one ambition is to be safe and find happiness, and who will benefit from the support they receive from the book. I know you will enjoy this anthology. On behalf of ChildLine I must thank everyone, contributors, cartoonists, publishers, the editor, Peter Langridge, whose talent and devotion make it possible, his wonderful assistant Marion Brett, and most of all you, for buying it. And the next time you ask a child "What do you want to be when you grow up, darling", watch out, you may be interviewing a future Pope.

NORMAN PACE

‘I always wanted to be a performer. One glance at a potty and I had to perform, which can still be embarrassing at dinner parties. It used to be “open a fridge door and Norman puts on a show,” and now I’m 36 it’s “open a fridge door and Norman puts on half a stone.’

GARETH HALE

‘When I was very young I wanted to be very hirsute. But as I reached my teens my burning ambition was to be a veterinary surgeon. Because I was no good at biology, I failed on both counts.’

KYLIE MINOGUE

‘I’ve really been an actress ever since I was a little girl. I appeared in television commercially when I was five and have worked ever since. Now I can combine all my favourite things, singing, dancing and acting in my career.’

NICK BERRY

‘Although I started acting at a very early age all I ever really wanted to be was a professional footballer and play for West Ham. One of the most brilliant things about being in *EastEnders* is that I got the chance to play in charity matches before two F.A. Cup Finals.’

THE ARCHBISHOP OF CANTERBURY

‘I grew up beside the sea in Liverpool. We used to watch the great ocean liners going up the Mersey. When it was foggy their fog horns kept me awake at night. My mother was away a lot because she was a hairdresser on a cruise ship which went round the world. So I dreamt about distant lands, romantic and magical places like China and India. My mother would bring back trinkets from bazaars in places like Cairo. “When I grow up,” I said, “I will travel the world.”’

KATIE BOYLE

‘I was passionate about Hollywood and its stars . . . especially Ginger Rogers . . . I was convinced I would be the greatest star of all! . . . I loved the clothes and when I looked in the mirror I was sure I could see the reflection of Ginger and Rita looking back at me! . . .’

ALAN TITCHMARSH

‘All the world was a stage when I was eight and I wanted to play all the parts. The trouble was my height. As the shortest boy in the school the only part I could get was Little Devil Doubt in the “Pace Egg” play at Easter. I can still remember the lines. “Here I am, Little Devil Doubt, if you don’t give me money, I’ll sweep you all out. Money I want and money I crave, if you don’t give me money I’ll send you to the grave.” If Jonathan Miller reads this, I’m available for auditions.’

HOUSE OF COMMONS
LONDON SW1A 0AA

The Office of the
Leader of The Opposition

My ambitions came and went. The one that lasted longest was to be a policeman. It seemed to me to be a good way of meeting people - with lots of sport and a fair bit of excitement thrown in, and eventually the prospect of being a canny, pipe-smoking Detective Inspector ....!

Yours sincerely

Neil

Neil Kinnock MP

KEEP
LEFT

BOB HOPE

‘I always knew I wanted to make people laugh, and recently a circus “buff” in Cleveland, Ohio sent me the following poem which he had “unearthed” . . . guess who the author was? I wrote it when I was eleven and I think it sums it all up.

THE CIRCUS

I dreamed I was a circus clown,
I wore a funny suit.
My shoes were blue, my nose was red,
I had a horn to toot.

But when I tried to take a step,
My feet refused to move,
I looked down to see the cause,
A lion held me in his paws.

I asked him please to let me go,
He growled and moved away.
“I’ll let you free to do a show
And come again another day.” ’

MAGNUS MAGNUSSON

‘It’s so long ago I can hardly remember! At various stages of my boyhood I wanted to be a writer, a preacher, an actor and a naturalist (my mother had just given me a pair of binoculars). Come to think of it, that’s more or less how it turned out!’

TONY GREGORY

‘When I was 10 I wired up two old turntables with a microphone and spent all my time pretending I was a radio D.J. I even made up jingles and commercials. Now when I'm interviewing pop stars on *Motormouth* I often think of those early days in my bedroom when I drove the neighbours mad by playing the same records over and over again!’

ADRIAN MILLS

‘When I was at school I wanted to work for the Midland Bank, and then I was told I needed "O" level maths, but the best I ever got was disqualified, or do I mean unclassified CSE maths.

However, my wonderful Careers Master suggested to my parents that he could have me working by 9.00 the following Monday as a peanut packer at the new KP Peanut factory in the Wirral. Thanks to a brilliant drama teacher who saw some potential where no-one else did, I was able to stay at school for another year, gain some extra "O" levels and a place at drama school in London.

After 12 years hard work as an actor in theatre, TV, radio and film, I've ended up working with dogs that say sausages, tight-rope walking hens, and show-jumping hamsters. Well *That's Life!*’

MIKE D'ABO

‘When I was about eight I used to play golf with my father and brother. My ambitions were always connected with sport. My fantasy was me on the 15th green about to putt a 70 footer with the commentary of Henry Longhurst in the background and, of course, I succeed to a rapturous applause,

My other fantasy involved me in my cricket whites saving the day for the team with a last minute run and dashing to the clubhouse to avoid the stampede.’

DOC COX

‘*When first I ever looked toward*
A "grown up" occupation
I hoped I'd join the British
Broadcasting Corporation.

And so, with tapes and microphones,
I played for many a year
And grew up joining Auntie Beeb,
A back-room engineer.

Then lovely Esther said to me,
"I'll give to you Doc Cox
The best job in the BBC."
(But she never mentioned the frocks!)’

SUSANNAH YORK

‘I wanted to be an actress, then I wanted to be a poet. Then the first person on the moon, then a doctor in a leper colony. Later, a clown, an explorer, a novelist, an actress again – and quite often along the line I wanted to be a gardener.’

STEPHEN HENDRY

‘As soon as my parents gave me a small snooker table for my twelfth birthday, I knew this was it – and I’ve been playing ever since.’

MICHAEL PALIN

‘I wanted to be something new every day. Indeed, some of my ambitions lasted only until lunchtime – marine biologist I think was one. Usually I found everything needed Latin or Advanced Maths, though you could probably bluff your way through an interview for rat-catcher with only a smattering of either.

Explorer was suitably vague, and involved getting a sun tan, so that was what I always wanted to be – well until Tuesday, anyway.’

MIKHAIL GORBACHOV

‘As a youngster I used to spend my holidays on my uncle’s farm and for a while my thoughts turned to an agricultural career but when I went to study Law at the Moscow State University, I very soon got involved in the world of politics and that set the seal on my future ambitions – incidentally it was at the Moscow State University that I met my wife Raisa.’

RAISA GORBACHOV

‘I am very flattered that you should ask about my childhood. I was brought up in a very literary world, my mother was a poet and I spent my early days reading all the great classics.

I went to the Moscow State University to study philosophy and there I met my husband Mikhail. Although still interested in philosophy my life is now so full I find little time to take a quiet moment and sit down with a book.’

BARRY HOWARD

‘I think I was the classic case of not knowing what I wanted to do. I just knew I wanted to be different. I was always an enthusiastic amateur actor especially at school. A girlfriend of mine in Nottingham then suggested I might try professional acting and, through this, I found an escape from my “ordinary” existence.’

GEORGIE FAME:

‘Having been captain of Leigh Central County secondary school’s rugby team, I desperately wanted to be captain of the town’s schoolboys rugby team. I made the team, but never captain. If I hadn’t become a professional singer I would have become a professional rugby league player.’

LENNY HENRY

Lenny

21st March, 1989

'When I was growing up I went through various stages of what I wanted to be. First of all I wanted to be a fireman because I liked red fire engines. Then I realised that being burnt or being suffocated by smoke probably wasn't a good career decision. Then with the advent of Muhammed Ali, or Cassius Clay as he was then known, I thought being a boxer would be glamorous. But then I quickly realised that black eyes and bruises were not for me! My final career choice was to be Elvis Presley but that job was taken, so I had to become a comedian.'

CAREERS No7
THE FIREMAN
STARTING A FIRE

BRUNO BROOKS

‘I have always had a love affair with birds and animals, and as a young boy I spent every spare moment building aviaries and breeding foreign birds. At one point I had over sixty exotic breeding birds. At this time I wanted to be a zoo keeper. Then I got interested in football and along with Garth Crooks and Adrian Heath I played with the Staffordshire County Intermediate football team.

While they went on to become famous football players, I started dee jaying at the local clubs. At this point I went through an "academic stage" and briefly flirted with the idea of becoming a chartered surveyor, but after a guest session as a DJ on Radio Stoke I realised that I had found my true vocation.’

DONNA McGRATH

‘My family were quite shocked when I announced at an early age that I intended to become a speech therapist. Then I changed my mind and wanted to become a physiotherapist because I really admired the work I saw them doing on my frequent visits to hospital. Soon after this I met a barrister and decided there and then that's what I would be and I am still hoping to become one or the other.’

Donna has overcome many handicaps to win the much coveted Best of British Youth Award organised by the 'Today' programme on Radio Four.’

TERRY HALL

‘My greatest ambition was to go into teaching. As a lad it looked the ideal profession — short hours and long holidays. However, it never happened! In fact, I became a ventriloquist at the age of 15, met Lenny the Lion in Blackpool in 1956 and we've been together ever since! Ironically, I have been able to realise my teaching ambition thanks to ventriloquism. A few years ago Lenny and I presented the educational series *Reading with Lenny*.’

NIK KERSHAW

‘I left school with no particular ambition except that I knew I wanted to sing, and after a particularly dreary two years working for my local county council I was fortunate enough to achieve my ambition.’

BARRY MCGUIGAN

‘As a young boy I always wanted to be a racing driver but as I grew older I realised I could not attain this. Being from a small town in Eire I did not have the money or the facilities to achieve this ambition.

So my attitude changed and since I was very interested in sport and always very successful I chose to become a boxer.

And ever since that day I wanted to achieve the highest honour of being World Champion, which I did achieve, but one ambition escaped me. As an amateur I wanted so much to become an Olympic Gold medalist, but unfortunately a bad decision when I reached the last sixteen in the qualifying rounds ended all hopes of that.’

RICHARD BAKER

I had several vague ambitions as a boy, but two were very persistent. I wanted alternately to be an actor and the captain of a ship. I did manage to do a lot of acting at school, starting as second lady-in-waiting in "A Midsummer Night's Dream", but command of a ship was more difficult to achieve. However, I did have a continuing fantasy about being the captain of the paddle steamer "Crested Eagle" and, whenever I called for my friends on the way to school, I was actually coming alongside the jetty to pick them up, although I don't think they ever knew it.

Best wishes

Richard Baker

ADRIENNE POSTA

‘Oh yes, I knew exactly what I wanted to be, or rather who: Marilyn Monroe! Blonde, beautifulf, funny, elegant, famous; in my eyes Marilyn had it all. However, I'm now quite happy with being me.’

EVE POLLARD

‘I always wanted to write, and thought I could make a living writing poetry. It came as a real blow when my career adviser informed me that this is a non-existent category in Yellow Pages.’

CHRIS BONNINGTON

‘A childhood ambition? . . . I'm not sure I had a clear cut idea of just what my future held, but I remember this quotation from William Blake and on reflection that it may have shaped my plans!

Great things are done when men and mountains meet.
This is not done by jostling in the street.’

PETER SIMON

‘When I was young all I wanted to be was a showjumper, or at least one of the men who rode them. Whenever I had any free time I would build a course in my mum's garden with buckets and with broom handles for jumps and create obstacles with the dustbin and some string.’

IVY BENSON

‘At five my father wanted me to be a concert pianist. At eight, after winning a Florrie Ford talent contest at the Leeds Empire, my mother wanted me to be a variety artist.

However, at ten after playing the saxophone and clarinet with Benny Goodman and Jimmy Dorsey and earning the nickname “Lady Be Good(man)” by Benny I decided it was a musician’s life for me, and have led my own all girl band ever since.’

MATTHEW BRODERICK

‘When I was very young I wanted to be a fireman, but I started acting at quite an early age and that sort of took over. My father was an actor and my mother an artist, so I was brought up in a very Bohemian household where painters, poets and people from the theatre would sit for hours discussing the arts. I guess it was inevitable that I would end up in a creative profession.’

ANNEKA RICE

‘From the age of about six I wanted to present Blue Peter. I reckoned that spending my days making and eating Granny’s Special Fudge Cake and playing with tortoises and collecting milk bottle tops would be some job.’

JAN LEEMING

JAN LEEMING

FOR

CHILDLINE

I always wanted to be an actress. As a young child my party piece was characterizing the story of 'Rumpelstiltzkin' dashing to and fro as both the dwarf and the miller's daughter. I first trod the boards officially at Greenwich Town Hall as a 'dancing tulip'.

GORDON JACKSON

‘I'd have loved to have been a doctor – especially a paediatrician! I think doctors and teachers are fabulous! I used to babysit my nephew in Glasgow. Now he's a successful surgeon there. I do envy him. Now I'm stuck with being an actor, because I can't do anything else!

I remember Spike Milligan singing(!) on TV many years ago:

What is my son going to be?
The Prime Minister?
Or the King of Italee?
Now he's a dustman in Chiswick!
Oh dearie, dearie me . . . ’

BOB MONKHOUSE

‘It was an illusion and the illusion was this: everything was bigger. No, I mean *everything*, not just houses and shops and grownups, but colours and flowers and journeys, especially journeys which seemed endless. "Are we there yet, Daddy?"

Funfairs were huge affairs that spread around you in infinite acres of noise and lights and exciting danger. Rainy days at home when you were ill stretched into eternity. Being an adult yourself was an unthinkably distant possibility. Every sound was louder, every game was grander, every pain unbearable.

As I've grown old, life has shrunk. Flavours have dulled. Surprises have turned into shocks. Days flutter by unsavoured. How can I recapture childhood when it was an illusion?

I have only one repeatable and precious way and even in this way I can regain only the echoes of that larger world. I can play upon the stage like a child and make the crowd laugh and laugh with them, sometimes helplessly like a child, and then, even though I am a sixty-one-year-old, I can almost catch the colours and sounds and silliness of those bigger years when I was little.’

HER MAJESTY THE QUEEN MOTHER

‘The Queen Mother is pleased to learn of all you are doing for children in trouble and conveys her best wishes for the success of your undertakings.’

BRIAN REDHEAD

‘When I was eight I read a story in *The Hotspur* about Scoop Mallory, ace reporter, and I decided there and then that that was what I wanted to be. From that day to this, which is more than half a century, I have never changed my mind.’

JIMMY JEWEL

‘My only interest as far back as I can remember has been with the theatre. My family was a theatrical one and my father was a north country comedian who also painted all his own scenery. My ambition was to follow in dad's footsteps and this is what I did.’

SIMON WILLIAMS

‘Does anyone remember *Champion — The Wonder Horse*? . . . Well, that's who I wanted to be, either him (or her?) or *Rin Tin Tin* the wonder dog . . . both of them childhood idols. Seems a bit strange looking back, but I was captivated by the intelligence of both animals and used to pretend I was them, hunting and chasing round the garden! Lord knows what the neighbours must have thought! Fortunately I grew out of it and became an actor.’

MICHAEL GRADE

‘I have a confession to make. Aged 46, I still harbour the same fantasy about my future career that obsessed me as a child. I want to conduct an orchestra. In those days, just any band would have done. Today, my ambition demands I front either the Duke Ellington orchestra, the Berlin Philharmonic orchestra or the pit at the Royal Opera House. I suppose I'm destined not to grow up.’

CARDEW ROBINSON

‘What did I want to be? A Red Indian Chief. However, after the headmaster had told me about the flowers and the bees, I quickly changed my ideas and decided when I grew up I would marry a geranium . . .

But seriously folks, I have always admired the underdog, that's why I support Wimbledon Football Club. As fate would have it I turned out to be a mundane comedian.’

PRUE LEITH

‘When I was ten I wanted to marry a horse. I had heard about an English woman who married a dog so it seemed perfectly sensible to me, and I prefer horses to people anyway.

At twelve I wanted to be a riding school teacher and at fifteen a movie star. I went to France when I was twenty and discovered I wanted to cook but it had never even occurred to me in my childhood to even boil an egg.’

SALLY THOMPSETT

‘At the age of 11 I was summoned to my headmaster’s office and asked what I intended to do with my life. I said “ a chef”. Although I am hopeless at cooking, it was and is my great love, although whatever I do in the kitchen it is always a total disaster. In fact, my friends joke there should be a government health warning over the door!

Having made the great decision, I was then offered five shillings by my brothers to go and audition for a summer show at our neighbourhood theatre. I went and by the end of the year found myself in a Lou Grade pantomime. I would still really love to be a chef.’

JOHN SESSIONS

‘I went to lots of schools as a boy, and soon found out that the way to deal with bullies was to make them laugh. So I spent most of my time dressing up and becoming other people. I suppose it was inevitable that I would become an actor . . . I was recently described as “ a frantic schizophrenic with mental indigestion and verbal diarrhoea”. Is that the same as being an actor?’

TONY BLACKBURN:

‘There is only one thing that I have ever, ever wanted to do in my whole life and I’m doing it . . . being a radio D.J. I started on pirate radio, moved to onshore radio and have been jamming the airways ever since.’

DAWN FRENCH

‘When I was growing up I wanted to be an air stewardess, because I’d been on a lot of plane flights since my Dad was in the RAF, and I noticed a lot of people didn’t eat their dinner! I thought if I was a stewardess I could scoff down everything that was left on the plates, behind the secret curtains. To show my devotion to this potential career I used to cut off the bottom of my Father’s trousers and wear it as a hat . . . *Thunderbirds* style. Thankfully, I’ve given up the habit of cutting off the ends of trousers, but I still manage to eat other people’s left-overs!’

GLORIA HUNNIFORD

‘When I was growing up in Portadown, County Armagh, Northern Ireland, I seemed to spend a lot of my time going to the movies. For such a small town it was incredible that it had three cinemas which changed their film programmes three times a week which meant we saw a lot of films.

I suppose it was inevitable that as an impressionable child watching this fantasy world on screen, I thought I would end up in the movies myself one day.

My giggling friends and myself would come home after the pictures as it was called then, and re-enact a lot of the scenes, whether it was trying to be a trapeze artist on a bar hanging from the yard door or, in my case, I always seemed to get the job of a maid servant brushing my mistress's hair.

Needless to say I neither had the looks or talent to take me on the silver scren!’

STUART OGG

‘I lived in India as a small boy and our house was surrounded by hills covered in beautiful flowers so, of course, I decided there and then I would be a horticulturalist. Now, as I approach my ninetieth year, I'm still “at it” in the garden and totally involved in the Delphinium Society and the Royal Horticultural Society of which I am president. Gardening continues to be my passion and long may it be so!’

EDWARD HARDWICKE

‘My first ambition was to be an engine driver. I was brought up in the age when all kids used to play with train sets, so engines were a great passion. But later I wanted to be a music conductor. I spent hours waving a stick over a gramophone record. I suppose it was the histrionics coming out! My real ambition later was to be a comic – Danny Kaye was a big hero of mine, and Sid Field, who was without question the funniest man I've ever seen’

Julia McKenzie

The first time I acted out 'Cinderella' with my grandmother, in front of her black-leaded stove, I think, as they say, my goose was cooked. So, apart from the occasional bend towards airline stewardess or nurse, its always been the Stage – or perhaps I just like dressing up.

FELICITY KENDAL

As a child
Wanted to be in a
circus a trapeze artist
or lion tamer then decided
I wanted to be an
actress working in the London
stage in Shakespeare and
doing new plays. So far so
good. But it wasn't
easy to start with!

From the Desk of Dame Edna

'Ever since I was a little girl in Australia, I always wanted to be a famous actress, though I never dreamt I would be as famous as I am. I always thought only very beautiful or rich people became famous and that fame came magically. Now I know that a lot of hard work is needed as well, but I am grateful for what has happened in my life and it is a wonderful job that I have – bringing laughter and happiness to other people.

A Joyous Heart Always.'

Dame Edna Everage

Don't throw this letter away Possum!
One day soon it will be a priceless collectors item.

WOODY ALLEN

‘As a child from Brooklyn, New York, the only ambition I had was to be someone else. My constant fantasy was that I'd be kidnapped.

I'd get into the car with the kidnappers, they'd drive me off and send a ransom note to my parents . . . My father had bad reading habits. He'd get into bed at night with the ransom note and read half of it, get drowsy and fall asleep . . . then he lent it out! Meanwhile the kidnappers take me to New Jersey, bound and gagged, and my parents finally realise that I'm kidnapped and they snap into action – they rent out my room! The ransom note says for my father to leave one thousand dollars in a hollow tree in New Jersey. He has no trouble raising a thousand dollars, but he gets a hernia carrying the hollow tree!

However, when I was in high school I used to write gags and sell them to a P.R. company who would then place them in gossip columns and attribute them to their "star" clients. After that I changed my name from Allen Stewart Konigsberg to Woody Allen. It sounded more American and less like a "lager", and I have been working ever since!’

NED SHERRIN

‘When I was growing up I wanted to be a soldier, a sailor, an engine driver, an actor, an author, a BBC announcer, an explorer, a comedian, a detective, a film star, Prime Minister, a Test cricketer, a football commentator and an all-purpose hero. Sadly very few of these ambitions have been realised.’

WET WET WET

GRAEME CLARK

‘I had a romantic idea of “Life on the Road” when I was young that made me want to constantly be travelling and in control of my own destiny which I suppose could translate into what I’m doing now — certainly the on the road bit which actually made me want to be a long distance lorry driver.’

TOM CUNNINGHAM

‘I always wanted to be a long distance lorry driver too! I thought it was so “glam” all that jumping into the cab and taking off down long straight roads. I’m sure it’s about as “glam” to lorry drivers as what we do is to us sometimes!’

NEIL MITCHELL

‘I don’t know what got into us at that particular age, but we all wanted to be lorry drivers — maybe it was watching *Smokey and the Bandit* or all those chocolate ads but we had an idea that it was our style. I’m glad we’re doing this though.’

MARTI PELLOW

‘The only time I remember being asked what I wanted to do for work was at the DHSS, but they didn’t have any jobs as shepherds on their books. I certainly didn’t want to be a long distance lorry driver but I always wanted to sing and I hope I always will.’

ARTHUR C. CLARKE

‘For over half a century I have been fascinated by the curious and mysterious workings of our planet. Although I trained as a scientist and an engineer it's the ghosts and poltergeists, and the supernatural elements of our world that I find more and more unexplainable as I grow older. So what did I want to be as a child? An investigator of the workings of our world.’

SIMON BRETT

‘I wanted to be a furniture remover until, when I was eight, our English teacher set us the homework of writing our own epitaphs. From then on my ambition was a rather unusual death, if only to justify these lines . . .
Here I lie, S. Brett by name
Killed by a lion I thought was tame.’

VINCE HILL

‘I was born in Coventry and certainly didn't want to be a singer. When my mother arranged singing lessons all my pals called me a cissy, and I used to pass them playing football while hiding my music in my jacket! Of course I appreciate it now, but at 15 all I wanted to do was work and earn money. I had a job in a bakery and for a couple of years I worked in a local coalmine. Later I started singing with a band and a couple of groups before becoming a solo singer. That was more years ago than I care to remember and I have always loved every minute of it.’

UNA STUBBS

‘Because I love children I wanted to be a Nanny. I thought I would find the job really challenging. However, my parents sent me to dancing school and there a whole new world opened up for me . . . so it was Bye Bye Kids, Hello High Kicks!’

MARJE PROOPS

‘No one believes me when I say that I always wanted to work on a newspaper. My mother said I started going on about it when I was aged five. I reckon she exaggerated. I must have been all of seven. I am also among the lucky few whose youthful ambitions have been fulfilled.’

ANNE CHARLESTON

‘I was one of those people who had a wild and imaginative childhood ambition . . . however, I'm afraid my dream was to be an actress. Playing Madge in *Neighbours* is really the fulfilment of that dream.’

SHEILA TRACEY

‘From the very first time I appeared in front of an audience when I was five years old singing *Coming Thro' the Rye* I wanted to be on the stage.’

PHILIP SCHOFIELD

‘I never had any doubts about what I wanted to be when I grew up. From the age of ten I decided that I wanted to work in television. However, when I was about five I went through an odd phase of wanting to be a gravedigger! I had decided though, to leave airholes with straws to the surface, just in case any of my “clients” still needed to breathe.’

THE LITTLE SLIDE MAKER
by
BARBARA CARTLAND
Aged five Dec. 1906

‘Once upon a time there was a little girl and her name was Mary. Now this little girl was very fond of making slides. Her father was the village doctor. One evening the doctor came home very late.

"Mr. Joe Catter stepped into a slide; poor old man," he said.

"I hope no slide will be made down Winters Hill or it will be a bad look-out for poor old Betsy Gray."

Then Mary felt very unhappy for it was just down Winters Hill she had made all her slides. That evening when she had been put to bed she got up and got a spade. When she got to the hill she found that the dirt on the side of the road was quite hard but she found some in the garden at the top of the Hill.’

SEVE BALLESTEROS

‘What did I want to be? A golfer of course! My family say my tenacity in this sport dominated my life and theirs! My guiding "Motto" then and now was:

The more I practise, the luckier I get.
The more I practise, the better I play golf!’

DEBBIE GREENWOOD

‘As a child my great heroine was Chris Evert, mainly because I was mad about tennis and had set my sights on one day playing at Wimbledon. Tennis is still my great love and I play whenever I can. I find it really relaxing. Occasionally I have little day dreams of walking on to the centre court. Fortunately I was one of those lucky children who was able to get to a court whenever I wanted to and I still have fond memories of warm summer evenings and that lovely sound of tennis balls being clonked across the net.’

SIR BERNARD LOVELL

‘As a child one of my favourite pastimes was to look at the sky on a dark, clear night. If the night was very dark I could just see a nebula in the constellation of Andromeda. That light had started on its journey two million years ago – when the earliest ancestors of man were beginning to evolve on earth. All this fuelled my imagination, and my drive to become an astronomer.’

JEANNETTE CHARLES

‘At school I played “Shylock”. The seed was sown. An actress I would be. After five years of repertory and disillusionment, I emigrated to Texas, I was twenty-three. Then I was mistaken for the Queen in a portrait . . .’

THE RT HON DR DAVID OWEN M.P.

HOUSE OF COMMONS
LONDON SW1A 0AA

‘When I was at school from age 7 to 11, I wanted to join the Navy and go to Dartmouth which then took young boys in at the age of 14. The Royal Navy then stopped the young cadet entry when I was still at school and by the time I was 18 when I could have joined, I had decided to become a doctor of medicine. I eventually became the Minister for the Navy and then the Minister of Health, so it could be said that I achieved my earlier ambitions but by a rather different route.’

Happy Reading.
Yours ever
David

DAVID OWEN

THE ARCHBISHOP OF YORK

‘I am not sure I could identify a childhood ambition but this is relevant, I hope, to all children:

Know what it is to be a child. It is to be something very different from the man of today. It is to have a spirit yet streaming from the waters of baptism, it is to believe in love, to believe in loveliness, to believe in belief.

It is to be so little that the elves can reach to whisper in your ear. It is to turn pumpkins into coaches, and mice into horses, lowness into loftiness and nothing into everything – for each child has his fairy godmother in his own soul.

It is to live in a nutshell and count yourself king of infinite space: it is to see the world in a grain of sand, heaven in a wild flower, to hold infinity in the palm of your hand and eternity in an hour.’

SUE LAWLEY

‘When I was really quite small I wanted to be a hospital almoner – a person who sorts out patients’ practical problems. It was an ambition born, I suspect, of being a busybody, even then. Ah, the joys of helping a mother of six about to have her bunions removed. Why, I could metamorphose her children and her house in a twinkling! And I’d have made her and many others downright miserable, I don’t doubt!’

SIR HARRY SECOMBE C.B.E.

‘I wanted to be a tap dancer and I practised really hard at it . . . unfortunately I had to give it up because I kept falling into the sink!’

RUBY WAX

‘As far back as I can remember I always wanted to present my own talk show. I called it *The Jenny Show*. Jenny being my star name; I always thought the name Ruby Wax was much too embarrassing. I did my show into a tape recorder and interviewed everyone who came to our front door. So a special guest would sometimes be the postman or someone selling Girl Scout cookies. I even did my own commercials and sang jingles. I wish my show now was half as good as, *The Jenny Show*.’

THE BISHOP OF LIVERPOOL

‘The two great passions in my life as a child were sport and religion and have continued to be so ever since, although I must say playing cricket has tended to take a bit of a back seat.’

GARY NUMAN

‘When I was young my biggest dream was to be a pilot. Not just a private pilot flying little aeroplanes for a hobby, I wanted to be an airline pilot or, even better, a fighter pilot in the Royal Air Force. I would sit and stare out of the classroom window watching the giant aeroplanes roaring through the air.

At air shows I would stand next to my dad and watch the fighter planes scream past. So much speed, so much power, the most exciting job in the world. I had no interest in money, I was only interested in machines. Aeroplanes were and still are the ultimate machine.’

NICK ROSS

'I wanted to be an engine-driver when I grew up. It seemed the most important and exciting job to do. That was in the age of steam when locomotives breathed and needed feeding, coaxing, taming like an animal, and when the rails were still butt-joined and tapped out urgent rhythms on the passing wheels. Then came welded tracks and diesels, and so I became a broadcaster.'

SIR PETER HALL

‘When I was seven or eight I wanted to design aeroplanes. I suppose this was my response to the war starting. At ten I wanted to be a musician — a conductor if possible, and if not, a concert pianist. At 12 I wanted to be an actor. And at 14 I wanted to be a director, and there I have stuck! I don't believe that at 14 I knew what a director was or what he did. But I knew that somebody made those wonderful things happen on stage and that's what I wanted to be.’

DON LUSHER

‘Whenever the chimney sweep came I was intrigued by the sight of his brushes, so my earliest ambition was to be a chimney sweep. Then I went through the usual boyhood stage of being fascinated by railway engines and switched track from chimney sweeping to engine driving. But I think that always at the back of my mind there was this voice urging me to make music.’

DEREK FOWLDES

‘Having overheard two rubbish collectors discussing how much they'd been given in tips, my first ambition was to be a dustman because the money seemed so good. Then, because we lived by a railway, I decided I would like to become a train driver. I left school at 15 (slightly regret that now) and while I was doing my national service a guy I met encouraged me to go into acting.’

KENNY BAKER

❛Like many young boys I was fascinated with building models of all types — ships, boats, especially engines. I just assumed that I would eventually go into engineering. However, my mother had other ideas and told me at a very early age, "You've got music in you." My mother was a very proficient piano player and teacher and my father was a semi-professional woodwind player so I guess it was inevitable that I would also follow in their footsteps.

At ten years old I was quite proficient at playing the piano, clarinet, violin and the accordion. Then I was introduced to the cornet and that was it.❜

"TEAZY WEAZY" RAYMONDE

❛My childhood ambition? . . . to be a violinist. I had lessons with the great Mantovani. All seemed to be going well until my father, who was a very innovative hairdresser, advised me to go to London's "Tin Pan Alley" just to see the number of out-of-work musicians who were there. This I did, and rapidly changed my mind deciding instead to become a hair stylist.❜

THE RIGHT HON. SIR EDWARD DU CANN KBE.

❛I have always been impressed and inspired by John Milton's poems and felt from a very early age that, like him, I would like to be of service to my countrymen. Hopefully I have carried this out to the best of my ability.❜

MARGARET THATCHER

‘I had an ambition as a child. I wanted to be part of the Indian Civil Service. I said: “I think Daddy if I manage to get to university” – *if,* it was a fantastic privilege in those days – “if I manage to get to university I think I'd like to go in the Indian Civil Service because I'd like to be able to do something for them.”’

CLIFF RICHARD

‘There was never a time when I wanted to be anything but a singer. I recently saw a photostat of a letter I wrote when I was 12 to a penfriend in Australia. “One day, when I grow up,” I said, “I want to be a famous singer.” I guess I've achieved the ambition . . . but I'm still waiting to grow up!’

GRANT BAYNHAM

‘Do you remember, when you were about ten, the sudden and petrifying realisation that you were an individual with the responsibility of one day paying for your own fish fingers and stamp collection? I do. At the same time, it occurred to me that somebody had the job of wrapping up the salt in those twists of blue paper which one used to find in crisp-packets. The fact that, failing all else, there exists a living at once so fascinating and so easy to make has kept me going ever since.’

DESMOND WILCOX

❛As a small boy during the second world war, I grew up in the Cotswold countryside. With my father away at war, I – as the eldest of three boys – helped pick and sell the apples from our orchard. I also bred rabbits and sold the meat to the local hospital, as many as 70 rabbits at a time. I received a scythe (for cutting grass to feed the rabbits) for my eleventh birthday present. But every spare moment I had I spent with horses, working in the local riding school.

I took fat little Thelwell girls out on leading reins. I shovelled mountains of manure, polished acres of leather and rode and jumped in every horse show and gymkhana, as the riding school sponsored "lad".

So, all I wanted, was to grow up and own my own riding school. Instead, the war ended, my father returned and the family went back to London . . . more than forty years on, I still wonder if I ever will own that riding school.❜

SU POLLARD

❛When I was younger, I was dead keen on being an archaeologist. I knew nothing about it, nor had any family connection, but I was fascinated by the idea of wearing a pith hat, kneeling in the desert heat, screaming "I've found one!" But the idea of studying for years on end put me off 'cos I wanted money for the disco, right then. Anyway, I still dream of doing it. Nowadays I don't dig up relics, I work with them! (just my little joke, my fellow artist's).❜

HIS HOLINESS POPE JOHN PAUL II

‘His Holiness assures you of his prayers for your good work on behalf of children in need, and he invokes upon you God’s abundant blessing.’

BJORN ULVACUS

‘I was born in Gothenburg in Sweden and received my first guitar when I was twelve. At that moment I knew what I wanted to do . . . make music . . . I started playing skiffle, progressed to Dixieland and then formed a folk group called *The West Bay Singers*. In 1966 I met Benny and soon afterwards we formed *ABBA* . . . we did pretty well! And I’m still singing and writing music, just what I always wanted to do!’

BENNY ANDERSON

‘My father and grandfather were fantastic musicians. I had my first accordion when I was six, 4 cm bellows and inlaid with gold and mother of pearl . . . every summer vacation we all three played together. When I was ten I got a piano, and by the age of fifteen I had formed a band. This band (*The Hep Stars*) had great success in Sweden with many hit records. After the group disbanded in 1966 I met Bjorn and the rest as they say is history.

What did I want to be when I grew up? . . . just what I am now!’

HELEN SHAPIRO

‘The only thing I have ever wanted to do is sing. My mother says that the moment I opened my mouth as a baby I sang something. While other girls at school talked of marriage, having children and working in shops or offices I knew that I would be a singer. That lasted until one week in the late Fifties when for some inexplicable reason I did a total about-turn and decided the only thing I wanted to be in life was an air hostess. This feeling lasted for seven days and then I decided to be a singer again!’

JONATHON PORRIT

‘At some very early stage, the vision of a Royal Canadian Mounted Policeman crept into my infantile imagination. Until I was eight or nine, I was just desperate to get over the Rockies, leap on one of those beautifully groomed horses and hunt down the baddies!’

MICHAEL ASPEL

‘It seems so long ago that I have almost forgotten when I wanted to be, but there are certain things that I remember, like favourite records, certain holidays and this little rhyme, which for some reason I have never forgotten and is perhaps one of my strongest memories from childhood:

God and the doctor we alike adore,
But only when in trouble, not before.
The trouble o'er, both are like requited,
God forgotten and the doctor slighted.

. . . funny the things you remember, isn't it!’

JEAN ALEXANDER

‘When I was about five years old, my father sometimes took the family to a variety theatre. Watching the various performers I was sure that one day I could do that! Later visits to the cinema confirmed this idea, and after my first experience of straight theatre, seeing John Gielgud in *Macbeth* my feet were firmly set on the long, hard road to becoming an actress. I have been very fortunate in achieving this ambition.’

LINDA LUSARDI

‘At fourteen I wanted to become a world class athlete and nearly did. I was district champion at running 100 metres and trained daily with an Olympic swimming team. I gave it all up when I discovered boys. I often wonder if I would have made the grade.’

MELVYN HAYES

‘Every day for the past fifty years, I've asked myself the same question, "What am I going to be when I grow up?" I always get the same answer, "Don't worry, you've got all the time in the world, the future will take care of itself." When I was a child the world was at war. I didn't know if I had a future. Now that I'm slightly older than a child, I'm an actor. My agent tells me "Melvyn, you still have all the time in the world . . . " but we call it availability.’

RAYMOND BRIGGS

When I was about 10 I wanted to be a reporter. By the time I was 13 this had been changed to a cartoonist. So the three things I have worked with since; writing, drawing and humour were already there in the infant brain. My family had been unskilled working people for generations, so where do these implanted programmes come from?

Raymond Briggs

THE PAUL McCARTNEY BAND

CHRIS WHITTEN

‘I guess I thought the most glamorous occupation in the world was an airline pilot. Unfortunately, I failed the ‘O’ levels I needed to achieve this ambition so at sixteen I went to music college in Leeds to study music. I had always enjoyed playing drums while at college and subsequently played with many jazz and pop groups.’

ROBBIE McINTOSH

‘At six years old I absolutely idolised The Beatles and my first LP A Hard Day’s Night just reinforced my ambition to play with them. When I was 11 I went through a phase of wanting to be a football player with Manchester United. At this point my hero became Georgie Best but was rapidly replaced when I discovered Chet Atkins and once more music became my great love. After dreaming of The Beatles, I now find myself in the fortunate position of playing with one!’

WIX

‘At school I was good at gymnastics, and at one point thought I would end up in a circus as an acrobat. After attending physical education college I was offered a job at my old school as the PE teacher. After giving it a great deal of thought I realised that I didn’t want to teach and instead I formed a group.’

SUZANNE YOUNGER

‘When I was small I suppose I was attracted to many of the things that all girls of my generation were attracted to. The main ones however were to be a television presenter and win a beauty contest. After winning the title Miss United Kingdom in 1989 I was offered the chance to present a television show, so to date I have achieved two of my childhood ambitions.’

JIM BOWEN

‘It's amazing, but from the earliest age I can remember I wanted to be a train driver! As it happens, I emptied dustbins in Burnley and then became a teacher before moving on to comedy and hosting *Bullseye*. But the really amazing thing about my childhood ambition is the fact that I now live in a converted railway station in the lake district, and the trains come past every day! What's more, I've actually had a go at "driving" a big, old-fashioned steam train. It proves that everything in life is possible if you put your mind to it.’

DICK VOSBURGH

‘In 1935 when I was six (not fair counting) I decided I'd be a radio performer when I grew up. Radio in my native USA is now practically defunct, but in Britain it's still very funct indeed, and I love doing it — although I still haven't grown up.’

PAUL NICHOLAS

‘Growing up in the fifties, all my heroes were in films, especially musicals. My favourite performer was a singing and dancing star called Gene Kelly. I wanted to be just like him. Well, I have grown up and have yet to do anything that begins to compare with my hero. However, I still dream and if I work hard enough, perhaps one day my dream will come true.’

FRANKIE HOWERD

‘As far back as I can remember, I seemed to be stage-struck. I loved going to the pictures and pantomime, listening to the radio, putting on little shows at the bottom of my garden — dressed in some of our parents’ clothes, which we borrowed when they weren’t looking.

I made my first stage appearance when I was 13 in the church dramatic society where they made me up to look middle aged, with the help of a beard and grey wig. And I played the part of the father of a lady who was old enough to be my mother.

The church warden told me then that I was going to be an actor and I thought this was the voice of God speaking, and so I was determined to carry out his wishes to become a dramatic actor. It seems that either I or the church warden got God’s message wrong since I ended up as a music hall clown. Neverthless, I thank God I did!’

SHEILA STEAFEL

‘Ahm gunna be en extriss . . . the gawky, rather odd-looking schoolgirl spoke with a South African accent . . . not surprising, for this was Johannesburg Girls’ High. Her teacher smiled. “Oh dear me, Sheila, I don’t think so. Now sit down, have another think, and I’ll ask you again later when you’ve thought of something more suitable.’

ERNIE WISE

‘I seem to remember three stages of what I wanted to be as a child.

First a railway engine-driver. My father worked on the railway as a signal lampman; he received very poor wages. My mother always used to say the train drivers earned over ten pounds a week so that was the future career for me.

Next I would like to have been a cricketer, because I loved the game so much.

Thirdly I wanted to be in films. Andy Hardy seemed to lead the sort of life I would like. Open top car, button-down shirts, Ann Rutherford who lived next door and a rich dad who was a judge.

So after that I was always on the road to Hollywood.’

SARAH BRIGHTMAN

‘When I was young, I dressed up in my mother’s evening gowns and tinsel which I placed on my head. I danced and sang for hours dreaming that I was an Opera Singer. There I was, two years ago in *Phantom of the Opera*, singing in an Opera House in a Victorian gown with a glittering crown on my head. It’s funny how some dreams come true!’

PATRICK MOORE

March 3

When I was six years old, my mother found and gave me by grandfather's 1894 Remington typewriter, which had come to light in our loft. I taught myself to type. At the age of 8 I acquired the 1908 Woodstock typewtiter on which I am writing this letter.

There and then I decided that I would become a writer.

I have.

Patrick Moore

ED STEWART

‘*When I grow up I want to be a guard upon a train*
And when I wave my little red flag
The train will be in vain

I wrote this at the grand old age of four, but when I realised the soot and smoke gets in your eyes, I turned my thoughts to less hazardous occupations.

During the forties I used to sit in front of our radiogram and pretend to be a radio presenter and make up my own scripts to accompany the programmes. My mother says she can still see me sitting in front of the radiogram, and that even then I used to love the sound of my own voice!’

JIM BOWEN

‘My first ambition was to be a teacher, but as I left school with no qualifications I settled for becoming a dustbin man. Eventually I went back to school in Burnley, got myself eight GCE’s and became a deputy headmaster. I supplemented my income by doing local comedy stints until I was discovered by the television programme *The Comedians*.’

JEREMY BRETT

‘My ambition was to be a jockey and ride in the Grand National. But I quickly realised I was going to be too big!’

SUSAN HAMPSHIRE

‘When I was growing up I wanted to be a nurse, but as I am dyslexic I found school work extremely difficult, especially Latin.

In those days Latin was essential for nursing, so I landed up an actress! I have always regretted not being a nurse, although probably patients should be grateful!’

JONATHAN DIMBLEBY

‘First of all I wanted to go into the Navy but my eyesight was not good enough to let me be a Captain, so I gave that up.

Then I wanted to be an actor. But I was not good enough. So I gave that up.

Then I wanted to be a professional horseman. And for three years I was, but decided there were limits to a life in the saddle. So I gave that up.

Then I wanted to be a farmer and trained accordingly but I couldn’t afford a farm and didn’t want to work for anyone else. So I gave that up.

Then I thought I would be an academic but in the process got caught up in politics and journalism. So I went to work for a newspaper.

The one thing I knew that I would not do was go into television. Which goes to show that you very rarely end up doing what you wanted to do in the beginning.’

FAITH BROWN

‘I had this amazing urge to fly. When I was about six or seven I was always being told off for walking in puddles. One day I said to my mother "I shall fly away. God won't tell me off and you don't need shoes in Heaven only slippers!"’

JEFFREY HOLLAND

‘I suppose I was what you would call an artistic child . . . at least I was the best “drawer” in my school. I always loved painting and was fascinated by the way real artists could produce images to make them look like colour photographs. You have to remember that when I was little most snaps were in black and white. My brother went on to pursue a career as a graphic designer while I went on to become an actor. A decision I’ve never regretted.’

SIR LAURENCE OLIVIER

‘To go on to the stage, and to be true to myself . . . I was always fascinated by the English language and reproduce for you the following quotation which has been an inspiration to me ever since those far off days of childhood:

We few, we happy few, we band of brothers;
For he today that sheds his blood with me
Shall be my brother; be he ne’er so vile,
This day shall gentle his condition:
And gentlemen in England now abed
Shall think themselves accursed they were not here,
And hold their manhoods cheap whiles and speaks
That fought with us upon Saint Crispin’s Day.’

Henry V, Shakespeare

DRUE WILLIAMS

‘When I was seven all I wanted to do was swim for England and to win. Every day I would get up at five and head for the local swimming baths with my long-suffering sister. After two hours practice we would come home and eat a huge breakfast then go to school. This regular routine went on for several years until I discovered other ways of using my energy! . . . girls and late nights! . . . although I became a Sussex champion I never raced for England but now I race every night in *Starlight Express*.’

ADRIAN MOORHOUSE

‘I have been splashing around since I was five years old but did not learn proper strokes until I was nine. My first real race came at eleven, so swimming has always been at the forefront of my life.

My secret life was in football, and George Best was my idol. I was given a Manchester United shirt one Christmas with a No. 11 and thought this was the start of something big. At Bradford Grammar School I played rugby until my asthma forced me to give this up. Fortunately the school had a swimming pool so once again I was able to continue with the first love of my life.

My ambition has always been to be the best swimmer in the world.’

RONNIE BARKER

What I wanted to be more than anything when I grew up was the owner of a toyshop – especially the one in the town that sold the lead soldiers. How bright, shining and beautiful they looked! I thought that soldiers were the most wonderful things.

Fortunately, later I preferred girls.

Ronnie Barker '89

HI-STAR GLIDER CO

‘When I was small there was only one thing I wanted to be. Bigger. That is still what I want to be. Then I would be the enormous person sitting in front of me at the theatre, instead of being the small person behind paying a fortune to watch dandruff.’

Lots of love,

Dukey.

RICHARD STILGOE

PETER O'BRIEN

‘Coming from an agricultural family in Australia, my first ambition was to be a vet, not a "Flying" vet like the character I now play in *The Flying Doctors*.’

JANET BROWN

‘I have always wanted to be on the stage and I am a very fortunate person because I have achieved my ambition, but if I had not entered the theatre I would have loved to be a window dresser!’

PETER LANGRIDGE

‘As a child all I ever wanted to be was someone else. It didn't matter who just as long as they didn't have to wash and brush their teeth in front of my father. In our house there was a bathroom, which my brothers used and a basin in my parents, room which I had to use and did I dread it! While my mum was downstairs cooking breakfast my father lay in bed and moaned at me for not washing behind my ears, my neck, whatever! . . . I used to wish that I could live in a house with my own bathroom and the only way of doing that, it seemed to me, was to grow up as someone else!

Of course eventually I had my own house and can do what I like in the bathroom. Even lie in the bath and write! . . . which is how I'm doing this . . . (sorry it's a bit soggy).’

LULU

When i was very young i really thought i would like to be a hairdresser! Would you believe the way things turn out!

You see i never imagined for one minute that someone like me – a wee lassie from an ordinary working-class Glaswegian background could ever really make a living from singing! So i thought i would work in a hairdressers in the daytime and sometimes sing with a band in the evenings!

And look what happened!

Love
Lulu

SIR RICHARD ATTENBOROUGH

‘I wanted to work in the theatre in whatever capacity I could. The fact that I have been lucky enough to be an actor, director and producer has realised all my childhood ambitions.’

SIR FITZROY MACLEAN

‘I can't truthfully say that as a youngster I ever had a direct goal in my mind. But whatever I do I am spurred on by a quotation taught to me by my father:

Always a little further
We shall go
It may be beyond that last blue mountain barred
with snow
Across that angry or that glimmering sea.’

BONNIE LANGFORD

‘As long ago as I can remember, all I ever really wanted to do was sing and dance. By the age of eight I was on Broadway in the musical *Gypsy* which was one of the greatest thrills of my life. I even met Liberace. I have spent the last twenty-one years trying to achieve my ambition and hopefully I will still be singing and dancing for my supper for a good many years to come.’

B B C

NEWS & CURRENT AFFAIRS

BRITISH BROADCASTING CORPORATION
TELEVISION NEWS
TELEVISION CENTRE
WOOD LANE
LONDON W12 7RJ
TELEPHONE: 01-743 8000
TELEX: 265781
CABLES: TELECASTS LONDON

There was a short time in my childhood (age about 7) when I wanted to be a saint when I grew up. This was in an early religious phase (long since passed) and was combined with my great admiration for a girl called Susan Pares (age about 12). I saw her give her only apple to a younger sister who'd lost hers. I was filled with admiration for this unselfish act and tried to imitate her. I soon realised that sainthood was an unrealistic target.

Anna.

ANNA FORD

THE NEWS
PROGRAMME
SAINT ANNA
by
GEORGE BERNARD SHAW
Ken Pyne

JEFFREY ARCHER

‘I never wanted to be an engine-driver as I always wanted to be the engine. I also wanted to Captain the English Cricket Team but discovered at an early age I simply hadn't got the talent. This was followed by the English Rugby Team with much the same result. Finally, I thought I would like a gold medal at the Olympics (100 metres) but didn't even manage to qualify for the British Team.

Ah well, there is always Prime Minister.’

RUTH MADOC

‘I always knew I wanted to be an actress and to this end I was encouraged by my teachers and my parents. Having won the heat of my local "Top Town" competition, I then went to Manchester for the finals and was really thrilled when I won.

At last it seemed as though I would achieve my ambition – little did I realise then the years of hard work and slogging round the country that would follow.

At the age of 15 I applied to RADA and to everyone's surprise, not least my own, I was accepted. It was only later I realised I was the youngest ever student admitted.

Coming from Wales it was almost inevitable that I should sing which is still the great love of my life.’

"Rovers Return"
c/o Coronation Street
Granada T.V.
Manchester.

9th March 1989.

Dear Esther,

All I ever wanted to be when I was growing up was an Actress.

So I never grew up.

My love to you all,

Julie Goodyear. xxx.

BRYAN ROBSON

‘My earliest memories are of kicking a football around in our back garden. I lived, breathed and ate football and continued to do so ever since. I can honestly say there has never been anything else I wanted to do other than to be involved with the game. Finding myself captain of a fabulous team like Manchester United and, of course, England is the highlight of my career.’

MADONNA

‘To dance! Sorry! But that’s all I ever wanted to be. Now I desperately want to be a really good actress, but in the beginning all I ever wanted to do was dance.’

ESTHER RANTZEN

‘When I was eight I decided to train myself for a career as a night club singer. I therefore learned all the words of every pop song, dressed myself in my mother’s blue velvet evening dress and practised for hours in the garden. It means I how have a unique repetoire of 1948 pop songs including such classics as *A, You’re Adorable* and *Candy Kisses*. The ambition persisted until I took singing lessons at the age of sixteen and discovered my voice had matured to a vibrant baritone. So unless I am reincarnated six feet tall with a hairy chest so that my physique suits my voice, I fear the nightclub cabaret circuit will be forever closed to me.’

FRED HARRISON

‘I left home at fifteen to join the Merchant Navy. Shortly afterwards the ship sank so I left to become a student and eventually arrived at the LSE in 1968 which closed during my second term. Someone, somewhere was trying to tell me something. Write was my interpretation and ten plays and several books later, I am still trying to work out what the hell is going on!’

THE BARON KNIGHTS
BILL COLEMAN

‘Growing up on a diet of adventure comics and war movies,the only ambition I ever had was to be a fighter pilot.

DUKE DUMOND

I wanted to be a printer like my dad!

PETE LONGFORD

As a child I was mad on horses and wanted, above all else, to be a jockey. But my mum's cooking was too good and I got too big, too fast.

BUTCH BAKER

My great hero when I was a little boy was "Dan Dare" from the famous *Eagle* comic series, so naturally that's what I wanted to be.

NIGEL REGRUM

My family tell me I used to drum with my rattles, then I graduated to drumming with spoons and forks, in fact, anything I could get my hands on. So I guess you could say drumming was all I ever wanted to do.’

HUGHIE GREEN

‘Hearing distant trains when young from my nursery, what else? I wanted to be an engine driver. One day a new sound landed in the field adjoining the house. An aeroplane. The exciting sound quickly made me forget the trains. I'd be a pilot or . . . wait a minute . . . my family's home, always filled with joyous theatre people who'd never stop entertaining, made me think again. I'd better do both. And for a lifetime have done so.’

SUE COOK

‘I wanted to be a famous singer when I grew up. I don’t think I thought out exactly what sort of songs I would sing, but I had a regular daydream that I was standing in the spotlight on stage, having given a brilliant performance. The audience were going wild stamping and applauding and cheering me . . . Ah well! . . .’

PENELOPE KEITH

‘When I was five I announced to my Mother one evening in the bath, that when I grew up I would be either an actress or a nun. My mother somewhat taken aback, said that nuns could not wear pretty clothes. I replied undaunted: “I’ll have to be an actress then”.’

SIMON MAYO

‘All I wanted to do when I was little was to be on the radio, or be a footballer or a train driver. I had a little plastic wind-up record player when I was seven and by the time I was ten I was well into radio. I used to have my own programme which had an audience of two! Me and my sister . . . she played all the jingles on her xylophone while I did dedications, requests and the weather forcasts!’

CHERYL BAKER

‘After seeing Sandi Shaw win the Eurovision Song Contest in 1967 I just knew that was what I wanted to do. I answered an advertisement in a music paper to join a group called “Coco” after leaving school, and my singing career then took off.’

EVE FERRET

‘From the very start I wanted to be a ballet dancer, but by the time I was eleven I wasn’t only taller than all the boys and girls in my school but I was overtaking some of the teachers as well, so that was out. Then my great scheme was to tile the Thames between Vauxhall Bridge and Waterloo Bridge so my friends and I could swim! At this time I was well into ice cream and that’s been the one constant thing in my life ever since. My love of ice cream combined with my love of flowers leads me to my ultimate ambition which is to open an ice cream and flower shop . . . as well as to continue acting, singing and dancing, of course.’

JONATHAN MORRIS

‘Before I left drama school and until I became a Boswell I had set my sights on being a navigator in the Merchant Navy. I suppose being born and bred in Liverpool it was inevitable that my career would be influenced by the sea. In those days big ships would come into the “Pool” and I would spend all my free time down at the docks. However, as I hate being wet or cold I now realise an acting career is infinitely preferable.’

THE RT. HON. DAVID STEEL, M.P.

HOUSE OF COMMONS
LONDON SW1A 0AA

When I was very young I wanted to be a long-distance lorry driver. This may have been because I was given a large hand-built wooden lorry one Christmas. As a student I had a holiday job ferrying new cars from the factory, long-distance, to their owners. As a result, I know I prefer being an MP.

CHRISTOPHER BIGGINS

‘When I was a child I only ever wanted to be one of three things, a vicar, a chef or an actor. Of these three being a chef was the first choice, mainly because I loved food (and still do!) and also because my favourite cook in the whole world was my Auntie Vi, and she still is! I've been really lucky in that I've managed to combine all three in my adult life. I've played several vicars in my career as an actor, I'm still eating and I've still got Auntie Vi . . . what more could a person ask for?’

CANNON & BALL

Bobby
‘I was born as the war was ending and was a teenager at the time of a musical revolution. My heroes were Elvis, Little Richard, Chuck Berry etc., and I therefore, wanted to be a rock and roll star.’

Tommy
‘When I was in short trousers I was very interest in all sports, especially football. I always wanted to play for England at Wembley. I realised my ambition a couple of years ago: I played at Wembley for a celebrity team on Cup Final day and scored a goal.’

TONY BENN

‘To be different! And many people would agree that I have succeeded.’

BARBARA WINDSOR

'as a child I was educated at a convent and I admired the nuns so much that I decided more than anything else I would be a nun when I grew up.

My mother thought this a childish whim. but did get slightly worried when she came home from work early one day and caught me practising to walk like a nun with a tea-towel on my head.

Good luck with the book.

+ Much love

Barbara Windsor

x

VIV RICHARDS:

❛Being born and raised on the beautiful island of Antigua, I spent my childhood swimming and playing cricket — apart from my family, the two great loves of my life. My dad was assistant governor of the local gaol so often our stumps were chalked on the wall and our matches accompanied by the cheers of the inmates . . . I am one of those lucky people who do for a living exactly what they always wanted to!❜

KEITH CHEGWIN

‘I had my heart set on being an architect but, as my teacher pointed out to me in no uncertain terms, my maths was not good enough! My career started at ten years old when I won a talent competition in Rhyll and was invited to join *Junior Showtime*. Of course I went and loved it, working with people like Bonnie Langford and Peter Simon. After *Junior Showtime* I went to drama school, then on to the BBC.’

MAGGIE PHILBIN

‘Like many young girls I wanted to run away and join the circus and fly through the air on a trapeze with the spotlight on me. However, having always loved animals, more than anything else I wanted to be a vet.

I gradually began to change my mind after working in a local theatre and Radio Leicester. On entering university, I had to decide which road to take – I chose Drama and English and hence my career began. I must say I often yearn for "what might have been" and maybe one day I may get the opportunity to put my experience with animals to good use and get "a proper job".’

JAYNE IRVING

‘All through childhood I was completely obsessed with the idea of becoming a showjumper. Unfortunately my parents could never afford to buy a pony and the nearest I came was achieving third in the sack race at the local gymkhana.’

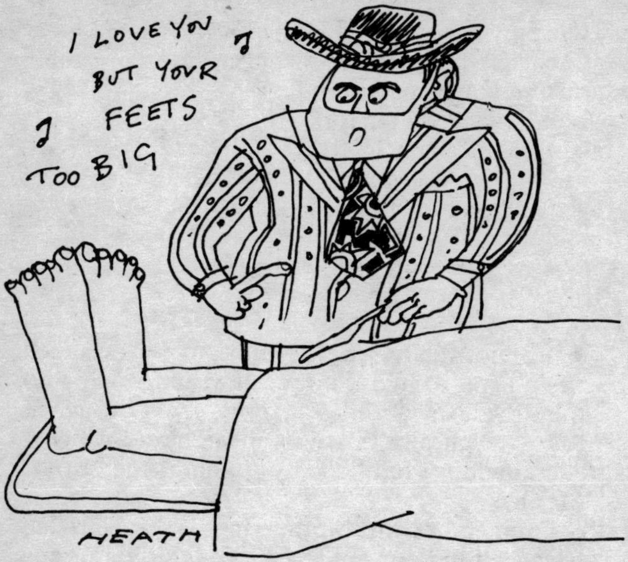

GEORGE MELLY

‘First and indeed last I wanted to be in some way famous. This was because my mother was so impressed by famous people. Definition of fame? Known by more people than you know. I then felt that perhaps I would like to be a *famous* surgeon until, in that it took me much longer than most children to learn to do up my shoelaces, I developed doubts as to whether I would be able to operate without automatically killing the patient.’

Rt. Hon Paddy Ashdown MP

HOUSE OF COMMONS
LONDON SW1A 0AA

‘I cannot really recall wanting to be too much when I was a child. I do recall wishing to go into the Royal Navy from, I am told, about the age of four, technically this was an ambition which I subsequently fulfilled by joining the Royal Marines.

I remember my Mother being very puzzled because I didn’t want to be a train driver or any of those usual things.’

Yours

Paddy

ANDREW LLOYD WEBBER

‘I hate to contribute a really boring story, but when I was a child I only wanted to be what I am now; a composer of musicals. I always had a great love of architecture and history and for a moment I wavered and thought that architecture might be my career, but the lure of the theatre proved irrestistible.’

DR. PETER ROWAN

‘To work in a vast factory. I certainly didn’t want to be a doctor – or even the Wide Awake TV-am children’s doctor – when I grew up. Doctors seemed a very odd crowd. You stuck your tongue out at them, and then they took your clothes off and stuck needles into you.’

RUBY MURRAY

‘I was born the youngest of four children and at the age of three my father knew I could hold a tune – so he used to stand me up on a table and let me sing. I went into the local church choir at four and I never really thought about anything else but singing – I loved show business and I still am in love with it.’

RICK ASTLEY

‘At a very early age, I decided that I wanted to be a musician. From that time on I devoted as much time as possible to this ambition because without determination and dedication it is difficult to succeed in any chosen walk of life.’

MICHAEL JACKSON

‘I was singing and dancing at the age of five, and so were my brothers and with my dads guidance we spent our days in school and our nights working so I never really had the time to do anything else. My great idol was Fred Astaire. I never wanted to do anything except to perform and put everything I had into it . . . I really hope this helps the book and send you my love.’

BENNY HILL

‘My grandfather used to take my brother and myself to the old Palace Theatre to see all the “saucy” reviews, with wonderful titles like *Night of Paris, Oh La La* and *Saucy Girls of 1902*. This was when I was eight. I always envied the principal comedian, surrounded by beautiful dancing girls, adored and laughed at by the ladies in the audience and definitely the centre of attraction. I thought . . . “That’s for me.”’

GAVIN CAMPBELL

'I wanted to be a Mountie in a scarlet tunic, with the black jodphurs, those wonderful riding boots, the epaulettes on the shoulders and the lanyard on the revolver and the big brown shiny holster and that hat which now seems to be extraordinarily ridiculous, but seemed to me then to be being really it. The black horse with the really neatly plaited mane and shining, creaky leather saddle wear and bright silver jingling bits. The Mountie always gets his man, and I imagine myself riding the rapids in one of those Canadian style canoes and plodding through the snow-covered silver birch forests to inspect my traps in the snow shoes that look like tennis rackets. And all because a little boy saw a little bit of the coronation and the little bit he saw was the Royal Canadian Mounted Police riding past.'

THE CARTOONISTS WERE . . .

Don 'Oz' Osmond	— Philip Schofield, Barry McGuigan, Michael Grade, Neil Kinnock, Richard Baker, Felicity Kendal.
Mike Webb	— Faith Brown
Ken Pyne	— Anna Ford and Susannah York
Charles Griffin	— Mikhail Gorbachov , Kylie Minogue, Su Pollard
Terry Parkes	— Paul Nicholas, Hughie Green, Lenny Henry
Mike Williams	— Nick Ross, Gavin Campbell